MW01105377

SURVIVING CULTURAL STRESS

HELP! MY DIET
IS A MESS

HOWARD MURAD, M.D.

Wisdom Waters Press
1000 Wilshire Blvd., #1500
Los Angeles, CA 90017-2457

Special discounts are available on quantity purchases by corporations, associations, and others. For details, contact the "Special Sales Department" at the address above.

Printed in China

ISBN-10: 1-939642-29-9
ISBN-13: 978-1-93964-229-5

First Edition

*Are you disappointed
in your appearance?*

*Do you find it impossible
to lose weight and keep it off?*

*If so, the reason may be Cultural Stress,
an insidious affliction of the heart and
mind that damages your overall well-
being. This dangerous malady is not
only a personal threat but is spreading
chaos throughout society. Here's how you
can survive this crisis and enjoy greater
health, happiness, and prosperity.*

SURVIVING CULTURAL STRESS

People aren't talking *to* each other anymore. They are talking *at* each other. They are frustrated and dismayed, and their anger is spilling out into the streets. Some people say they can hardly recognize the world we're living in today.

What on earth is happening to us? The problem is at once quite simple and extremely complex. It's stress. But not that old-fashioned stress you feel when you're taking an exam, under pressure at work, or in the midst of an argument with a friend. No, this stress is a different thing altogether. It's *seismic*. Its sources run deep like the fault lines that produce major earthquakes. This new **Cultural Stress** is terribly dangerous and debilitating, and it's afflicting all of us.

Is Cultural Stress for real? Science says it is and it's deadly. More people die each year from stress-related illnesses than from any other cause. Most don't even know they are suffering from Cultural Stress, making it a silent killer. It's stalking you, and if you have doubts about that, you'd better check your cell phone. You might have missed a text.

The communications explosion of recent decades has wrought social and political changes no less potent and stressful than those brought on by the industrial revolution two centuries ago. The jangling of cell phones is by no means the only way our 21st-century digital culture is poisoning us and our global society with stress. Today, information moves at the speed of light and there's just no way to keep up with it. We want to answer every ring, text, and email and accomplish everything our culture demands of us. We strive for perfection, which, like a mirage, is always just out of reach. As a result we feel at a loss, inadequate, overburdened, and cut off from our fellow human beings—even from nature itself.

In short, cultural stress is the constant, pervasive, and ever-increasing stress of modern living. It results not only from a dependency on digital forms of communication but from many other factors such as the growing financial pressures on middle-class families, increasing expectations at work and at home, and a continuing surge in the rules and regulations we are expected to follow. It produces a condition referred to as Cultural Stress Anxiety Disorder, which is associated with poor dietary habits, a sedentary lifestyle, loneliness, feelings of anger, and a diminished sense of self-worth.

What to do? Often, we can't change the factors that cause cultural stress, but we can change how we respond to them. We have to break out of our isolation, put away our perfectionism, win back the innocence and robust health of our youth, and start living again—*really* living. It's just as simple as that.

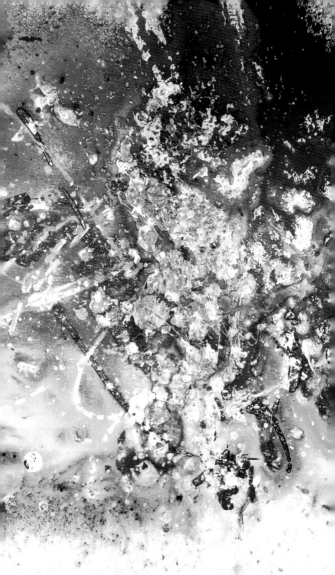

HELP! MY DIET IS A MESS

Sandra was carrying more weight than any physician was likely to recommend. I'm not going to say how many pounds I thought she needed to lose, because I don't think numbers are the point when it comes to problems with weight. They're not really part of the solution either, and I hope that after you read this little book you'll agree.

I met Sandra when she visited our offices in Manhattan Beach, California, and volunteered to participate in one of our research projects. The purpose of this particular project was to study the impact of Cultural Stress on individuals and to seek effective treatments. Sandra said she was experiencing a great deal of stress and believed that most of it was related to her weight problems.

"I've tried everything," she said. "You wouldn't believe how many different diet plans I've followed."

"Probably, I would believe it," I replied.

"Twelve of them!" she said. "An even dozen, and those are only the ones that I've taken seriously. I've tried low-carbohydrate diets and high-carbohydrate diets, low-fat diets, and high-protein diets. I've tried diets that let you have bacon and eggs for breakfast, but no bread or jam. Diets that consist only of milk shakes. Diets that require you to count every single calorie and budget them on a little hand calculator…"

"And how has all of that worked out for you?" I asked, already knowing the answer.

"Sometimes I've lost a little weight, but I always gain it back after a couple of months," she replied. "A few times, I gained back more than I lost! It has really been very stressful."

We talked for a while about stress, and I suggested that stress might be the primary *cause* rather than just the painful effect of her weight-loss problems. Stress can damage and dehydrate cells, emptying them of vital nutrients and causing the body to crave high-calorie foods. Stress often causes us to eat compulsively in ways that have little or nothing to do with true nutrition. And it can rob us of the sleep we need to lead a healthy life. Lack of sleep produces hormonal changes in the body that can cause us to eat more and feel less satisfied when we eat.

We discussed the stress factors in Sandra's daily life, and there were plenty of them. She had a high-pressure job as director of human resources at a sizeable firm, and getting to work each day required a long commute over highways jammed with traffic. She had what she described as a "challenging marriage" that didn't always provide the companionship, support, and satisfaction she wanted. With all these demands on her physical and emotional resources, Sandra struggled to meet the needs of her two teenagers. And that made her feel even worse.

"That's a heavy load of stress for anyone to carry," I said. "And likely those are only the most obvious sources of stress. Most people aren't even aware of the Cultural Stress placed on them each and every day."

I explained that Cultural Stress is an ever-present background stress somewhat like the constant noise one hears in a big city. It never completely goes away, so we tend to take it for granted. This makes it particularly dangerous, even more so because most of us do little or nothing to manage or control it.

As I told Sandra, Cultural Stress was the subject of our study and, should she decide to participate, perhaps she would learn more about how it was affecting her life. She was very interested and wanted to help with our research. As part of the study process we obtained key health indicators such as her blood pressure, cell hydration levels and, of course, weight. We also gave her a set of cards. On each card was printed a brief insight or affirmation such as the following:

Why have a bad day
when you can have a good day?

If it's no big deal,
don't make a big deal about it.

Beware of creating your own stress.

Be imperfect, live longer.

Be thrilled with who you are.

Forgive yourself.

*Your harshest critics are really
very critical of themselves—not you.*

Give yourself permission to be successful.

Dance even though you don't hear the music.

Happiness resides within.

*The best is yet to come—
you just have to let it enter.*

Most of these insights are not directly related to stress, but they are related to how we as individuals respond to various stress factors. We hoped they would encourage study participants to think about the stresses they were experiencing and the physical or personal problems these may be causing.

As we did with our other study volunteers, we asked Sandra to read through the cards at least once each day or whenever she felt particularly stressed. We also asked her to keep a journal. Later, if she felt comfortable doing so, she could share her journal entries with us.

The medical information we obtained from Sandra, particularly her blood pressure, raised some concerns, and I recommended she see her personal physician about this very soon. I also suggested she ask her doctor for help with her weight problems. Before she left, I gave her a signed copy of my book *Conquering Cultural Stress* (Wisdom Waters, 2015) pointing out that it includes an extensive chapter on how to maintain a healthy, youth-building diet.

DIETARY WASTELAND

For days after her visit, I couldn't get Sandra and her diet frustrations out of my mind. While her experience may seem extreme—12 diet plan failures is a lot—I have heard many stories like hers over the years. When I give talks on our Inclusive Health program, people often come up to me afterward and ask what they can do about their weight. Some are practically in tears.

Unfortunately, I don't have a quick fix to offer them. After all, no one does. I tell them the truth: Gimmick diets almost never work. What you need is a *healthy* diet, one based primarily on fresh, uncooked fruits and vegetables and embryonic foods such as seeds, nuts, and eggs. Such a diet will help you properly hydrate your cells while maintaining proper nutrition— and if you do that, your weight problems will very likely take care of themselves. Eating well doesn't have to be boring. Not at all! Healthy food can be *delicious* food. And eating healthy doesn't have to be difficult... though it does require a conscious shift.

In this era of Cultural Stress, eating properly can be quite difficult since there are dietary minefields almost everywhere we go. Imagine you are accompanying me on a drive around suburban Los Angeles. This is a beautiful city, especially during the early evening when everything sparkles. Like Dorothy's Emerald City of Oz, Los Angeles at night is all about light and color. Unfortunately, much of the color and visual excitement out here on the boulevards is evidence that we are trekking through a dietary wasteland. Wherever you look, bright signs beckon motorists, urging them to stop in or pull up to the drive-through for a quick fix of edible stress: burgers and fries, tacos, fried fish... and fried everything else! This stuff is loaded with fat and sodium, nearly devoid of nutritional value and, perhaps worst of all, intended to be eaten on the run. I'd venture a guess that there's a strip near your hometown that's just like this and you've eaten behind your steering wheel on many occasions.

Better food can be found at many, if not most, of the city's more conventional (and sometimes unconventional) eating spots where it can be enjoyed in a far more relaxed atmosphere. Culinary experts and travel writers rank more than a few Los Angeles restaurants among the finest in the world. There are even mobile food trucks here that serve up world-class entrees that can be savored curbside, in your car, or taken home to be the centerpiece of a quiet dinner.

These meals can be and often are delicious… but are they healthy? They *can* be, but most restaurant meals are sadly lacking in a key ingredient that must be a part of any truly healthy diet: the raw fruits and vegetables that provide the structural water needed to properly hydrate cells. Because liquids generally pass right through the body without being absorbed by the cells, you can't get the water you need just by drinking it. You need to eat your water. And, for healthy ingredients that are rich in water, you generally have to go shopping.

Not all markets and grocery stores are equal. If you want to be presented with only the highest-quality fresh and organic foods and ingredients, you'll get what you pay for. You know the type of store I mean. These places can inspire you to eat a wider variety of healthy foods. But even here health threats may be lurking. For instance, the prepared foods in organic markets may be laced with salt and literally

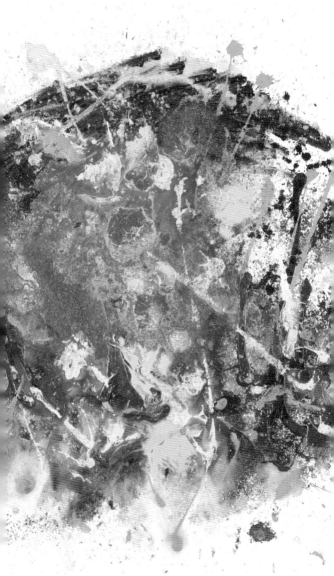

swimming in oil. You'll be far better off invest-ing in the hand-picked fruits and organically grown vegetables temptingly displayed in the produce section. Or, with a little more effort and less cost, you can be a careful consumer at any ordinary supermarket.

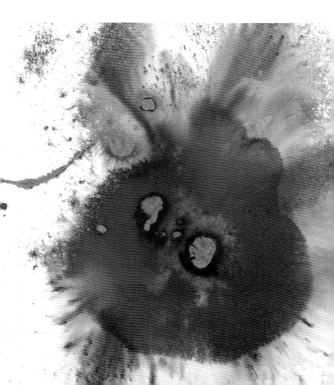

EATING A LOW-STRESS DIET

In recent years, we've heard a lot about the value of eating organic, whole, and "healthy" foods that are low in fat and relatively high in so-called "good carbohydrates." But even if you carefully follow a diet based on these principles, you could still be missing out on vital nutrients your body urgently requires. How many people do you know who, like Sandra, attempt to lose weight by restricting or eliminating certain foods while opting for supposedly healthy alternatives? Do they manage to lose weight and keep it off over the long term? Most people do not.

Surveys indicate that approximately 80 percent of Americans try very hard to maintain what they believe to be a healthy diet. Medical research proves that only about 10 percent of us are successful. The majority of us are overweight or obese and chronically dehydrated. How is this possible?

Many, if not most, of the popular diets we try to follow strictly limit fats, emphasize protein, or push particular types of carbohydrate. And for one reason or another they don't seem to work. This strongly suggests that we're focusing on the wrong things.

What if we simply ate foods that feed our cellular membranes and encourage healthy levels of cellular water? My own research and experience with thousands of patients have shown me that we'd have far better results.

While weight loss is definitely a beneficial objective for most of us, it should not be our primary goal. What we need is to put water back into our cells and keep it there. If we succeed in this, our weight problems are likely to take care of themselves. To hydrate our cells, we must flood our body with the nutrients required to strengthen cell membranes and connective tissues so that they hold water without allowing it to leak away. By retaining water in your cells, you can maximize and even accelerate your metabolism, sculpt stronger muscles, lift your mood, burn unwanted fat, and begin to look—and live—younger. And you will likely lose weight.

Understandably, people spend a lot of time thinking about food—what to have for lunch, what to cook for dinner, or how to sneak in a sinfully delicious desert. Advertisers know this and make billions in catering to our food fantasies. As a result, the average American is exposed to about 3,900 calories a day through TV, radio, and print advertisements. Sometimes, foods advertised look better on television or in magazines than they actually taste. But the more we see food, the more we want it. Just *thinking* about food increases the likelihood that you'll eat it. But there's good news as well: The same tendencies also relate to healthy foods. If you see a great looking salad, you're more likely to think about it, want it, and eat it.

I suggest that you mentally focus on foods that are good for you. Try to shop only in markets that emphasize fresh foods and promote healthy eating habits. And whatever you do, try very hard to avoid fast foods—they're not only nutritionally disastrous but closely associated with a high-stress lifestyle.

As I told Sandra during our initial meeting, maintaining a healthy weight may have as much or more to do with how we live as with what we eat. Exercise plays a vital role, as does a rich and fulfilling social life. Social interactions should be primarily face to face and person to person. Social media, text, and telephone contacts won't do much to relieve the constant isolation that generates Cultural Stress. In fact, social media and the general overuse of computers and cell phones are major stress factors themselves. When people stay up to all hours answering emails and keeping in touch with their social network they don't have time for a true social life and, critically, they don't get enough sleep.

Yet another factor that drives Cultural Stress is the constant drumbeat of terrible news in the media. It can leave us feeling anxious and depressed. Often it's better just to turn it off and recharge our engines the old fashioned way— with friends and creative pursuits. If we can successfully deal with all these 21st-century stress factors, or even a few of them, I believe we'll all be much healthier and happier as a result.

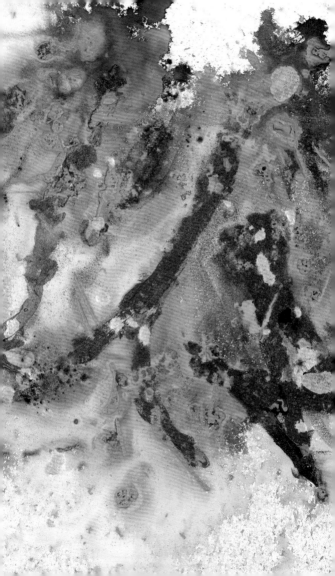

EATING A WHOLE-LIFE DIET

Sandra proved to be one of our best study volunteers ever. She followed our instructions closely and responded very well to the insights. When she made her follow-up visit to our research center a few weeks into the study process, her health indicators showed considerable improvement. Her blood pressure was lower and her cell hydration levels much improved. And, likely most encouraging for her, she had dropped a few pounds. She also looked much more relaxed. It was almost as if she had been scurrying around in circles and had finally given herself permission to stand still and take a deep breath.

The study journal Sandra shared with us was packed with entries, literally hundreds of them. Her diary-style observations showed that she had begun to reexamine the way she interacted with her associates at work, with her family, and with everything around her. She had resolved to get much more exercise, particularly outdoor exercise, and to take whatever steps she could to cut down on her exposure to Cultural Stress.

To accomplish this she had decided, she said, to put herself on a "whole-life diet." Sandra explained that the reason all her earlier diet plans had failed had become clear to her. Those diets only affected what she ate and when. Sandra had become convinced that she needed a plan that would engage other aspects of her life—work, family, social relationships, and the daily pressures and disruptions of life in the era of Cultural Stress. How did she think her new approach would work? She said she didn't know for sure, but she was optimistic.

Before she left, I counseled her on the purely dietary aspects of her new plan. I told her she didn't have to be overly strict to eat a healthy diet. She should think in terms of *adding* healthy foods to her diet rather than subtracting unhealthy ones. The important thing was to emphasize fresh fruits, vegetables, and embryonic foods such as nuts and eggs. If she did that about 80 percent of the time, she could let herself go the other 20 percent and she'd be fine. I urged her to craft her diet to her own tastes. She should enjoy her food and, if at all possible, enjoy it with others.

As Sandra went out the door, I wished her the best. I wished her good luck as well although I did not do so verbally. I felt she was headed in a very good direction and didn't want her to think that I thought otherwise. However, hers was a long-term project—living life well always is—so it was impossible to say for sure how it would turn out.

Sandra was not a regular patient in my dermatology practice, so I could not be certain that I would ever see her again. As it happened, I did, about a year later. In a marvelously appropriate coincidence we encountered one another in the produce section of a supermarket that sold mostly organic foods.

I was selecting avocados intended as a key attraction of a salad I would make later that evening. They had just gotten in a fresh shipment and these were especially ripe and luscious. An attractive lady standing beside me apparently thought so, too.

"Those are really great looking avocados, Dr. Murad," she said.

"Yes, they are," I replied, but was momentarily at a disadvantage.

"I'm Sandra," she said. "From the study?"

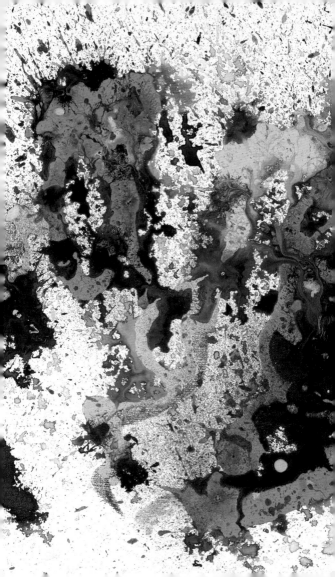

"Of course, Sandra," I said. "It's so wonderful to see you!"

And it *was* wonderful. She had changed so much—all for the better—that it's no surprise I didn't immediately recognize her. She seemed so much happier and relaxed, and she'd lost so much weight that she might have been a completely different person. But she wasn't. She was just a much healthier and happier version of her former self.

I wanted to ask how her "whole-life diet" had worked out but struggled to find the right words. After all, why ask? The answer was obvious. Finally, I settled on the following.

"Life is good?" I asked.

"It's good."

For more information on healthy eating along with recipes for temptingly healthful and delicious water-rich meals, get a copy of my book *Conquering Cultural Stress* (Wisdom Waters, 2015) or visit murad.com.

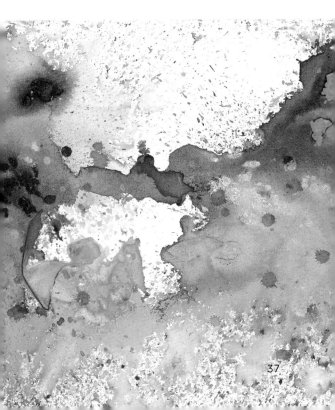

HELPFUL THOUGHTS
FOR HEALTHY LIVING

occasionally have what I believe to be a meaningful insight into the human quest for health
and happiness and I write it down. I can't say
exactly how many of them I've collected over
time. Probably there are more than 500 of them
in all and I keep adding to the number. Why do
this? Well, in part I do it for the same reason
any one writes—to express myself. But I also
sincerely hope that people will read the insights,
take one or two of them to heart, and perhaps
live a more fulfilling life as a result.

When patients visit my office to take part in our
Inclusive Health program, also known as the

Connected Beauty program, or participate in one of our studies, I share several of the insights with them. If they find any of them especially meaningful, I make copies for them. I never try to define the insights for patients or study participants. It's up to them to decide what the words mean. I believe each person responds to the insights in their own unique fashion, and if they are to be of any real benefit, it has to be that way.

Even so, many of the insights I share with patients are related in one way or another. They all have in common a central set of ideas: You can change your life for the better, happiness is really a byproduct of how you approach the challenges of living, and youthfulness stays with you when you focus less on the passing of years and more on all that is possible in each new day. An increasing number of the insights I've composed in recent years address the subject of stress and the crushing burden it has

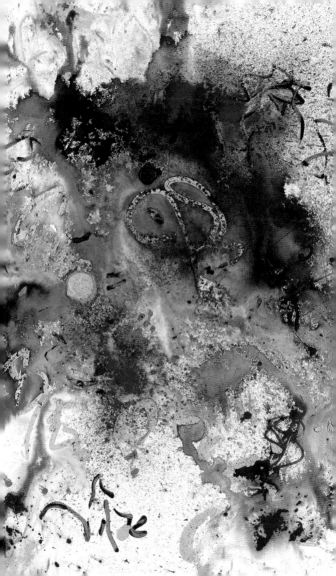

begun to place on Americans and people everywhere. The following also reference diet and the need to eat more water-rich foods.

Eat your medicine.

Before there was medicine there was food.

The ultimate cellular need is water.

Healthy, hydrated cells are the key to ageless skin and a healthy body.

Eat your water.

Splurge often.

Detoxify your body with plants.

Before there was medicine there was food, before there was food there was chocolate.

A healthy breakfast while vegging out
keeps the doctor away.

Eat to hydrate your brain,
allowing happiness to enter.

If one or more of these insights appeal to you or touch something within you, make them part of your life. Hundreds more are available on Murad.com and in *Creating a Healthy Life, Conquering Cultural Stress,* and my other books. Daily insights accompanied by inspirational artwork can be found at the Apple App Store by entering Dr. Murad's Inspirations.

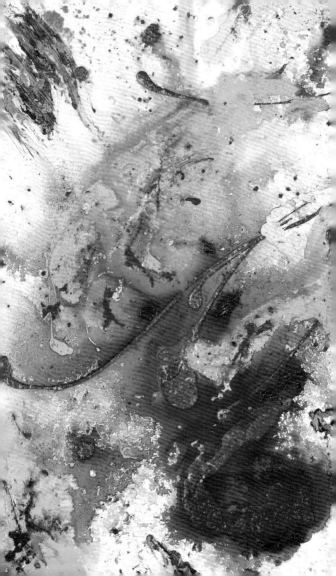

ABOUT THE ART

When I create paintings like the ones you see in this book, I make a few marks on canvas, add some colors, and spray them with water. The water interacts with the colors in a more or less random way, and this often carries the artwork in a totally unexpected direction. How's it going to turn out? I don't know.

My life has been like that too. Some might be surprised to learn that I started out thinking I wanted to be an engineer. When that didn't work out for me, I went into pharmacy and that, in turn, led me into medicine. Whatever happened along the way, I always felt life was carrying me somewhere. Life is a canvas, you see. You make your mark on it and then flow with it.

If you allow it to flow in a way that makes sense, your life will be a work of art.

I didn't start painting until 2008 when retinal surgery forced me to spend a rather challenging month always looking down. My wife, Loralee, suggested I try my hand at art to help me pass the time. I followed her advice and found that expressing myself with color on canvas was far more invigorating than I had ever imagined. I truly believe the painting helped me heal faster, and after that experience, I began to incorporate art into my overall skincare and general health philosophies. Along with an emphasis on personal creativity, my approach includes a diet rich in water and whole foods, appropriate skincare products, targeted supplements, rest, and plenty of exercise.

It also includes a positive attitude. You don't need me to tell you that happy people are more attractive. There is an emotional component

to both your appearance and your health, and when you are creative your emotions are allowed to run free. If you have an engaging outlet for your natural creativity, you will sleep better, be more vibrant, and smile a lot more.

When I consult with patients, we don't just talk about individual skin conditions. These are always linked to other problems and concerns, so we discuss a whole range of health-related issues. We also discuss various ways people can express themselves creatively. What this comes down to in the end is finding ways to access their inner toddler, to look at the world around them the same way they did when they were just two or three years old. The freedom that comes with rediscovering that fresh, child-like outlook has benefits that extend far beyond art. It can improve every aspect of our existence, changing life into the youthful adventure it was always meant to be. That is why I always try to send my patients home with a plan that takes personal creativity into consideration. Art therapy works, and more and more hospitals and clinics are using it to improve both the emotional and physical health of their patients. I do the same in my medical practice and my writing. I especially encourage you to let the light of youth enter and make your own life a work of art.

49

DR. HOWARD MURAD'S INCLUSIVE HEALTH APPROACH

A prominent Los Angeles physician, Dr. Howard Murad has successfully treated more than 50,000 patients. Drawing on his training in both pharmacy and medicine, he has developed a popular and highly effective line of skincare products that has won praise from health and beauty conscious people everywhere. A practitioner not just of medicine but of the philosophy of health, he has written dozens of books and articles that have earned him a worldwide reputation as an authority on slowing the aging process.

Dr. Murad's approach to medicine is unique. It involves a concept he calls **Inclusive Health**. Sometimes this groundbreaking concept is referred to as Connected Health or Connected Beauty, but all three terms basically mean the same thing: Our skin, internal organs, diet, lifestyle, and fundamental outlook are very closely linked.

An alternative to traditional medical practice with its emphasis on the "spot treatment" of individual conditions or illnesses, the Inclusive Health philosophy is centered on the idea that healthy, beautiful skin is a reflection of how you live your life. Every aspect of your life directly affects cellular hydration and the health of every cell in your body. That is why Dr. Murad believes there is a powerful, yet often overlooked, connection between the mind, body, and skin. This link is the essence of the Inclusive Health concept that he has made the foundation of his whole-person approach to beauty, health, and well-being. It is intended to inspire you to take care of your skin—not only with his highly effective products but also with proper nutrition, physical activity, and stress management.

Years of painstaking research and experience with thousands of patients have shown Dr. Murad that human health and happiness are, in fact, directly linked to the ability of cells to retain water. A poor diet and the stress of day-to-day living can damage the all-important membranes that form cell walls. Over time, these membranes become broken and porous, causing the cells to leak water and lose vitality. This, in turn, leads to accelerated aging and a wide variety of diseases and syndromes.

In his bestseller *The Water Secret*, Dr. Murad explained how to stop this process—and reverse it—through Inclusive or Connected Healthcare. This approach has three essential components. The first is a healthy diet that emphasizes raw fruits and vegetables. This allows us to literally eat the water our cells need to survive. Proper hydration levels cannot be maintained merely by drinking liquids, which pass right through our body while providing very little benefit. Instead, we must hydrate our cells by eating water-rich foods. The second component involves good skincare practices, and the third an overall reduction in stress combined with a more youthful and creative outlook on life.

The third component, which emphasizes our emotional state, may be the hardest part of the Inclusive Health treatment process for people to adopt. The breakneck pace of modern life with its freeways, computers, cell phones, and fast-paced living places upon us an enormous amount of what Dr. Murad describes as Cultural Stress. To deal with this runaway stress, we live increasingly structured lives that are less and less open to the free play and creativity that make life worth living.

We can choose not to live this way.

Of course, reducing stress and embracing a more youthful outlook often involves major shifts in lifestyle: changes in jobs, accommodations, locales, hobbies, habits, and relationships. It may even require a complete personal transformation of the sort sometimes identified with a single galvanizing moment of self-awareness. You may experience a transforming moment like that while walking on a beach, creating a work of art, driving through the countryside, or maybe just stretching your arms after a long night's sleep. Who can say?

BE HEALTHY, HAPPY, AND SUCCESSFUL!

Improve your life with these and other exciting Howard Murad titles now available on your favorite eBook platform. Handsome gift book versions can be purchased at Amazon.com and other book outlets. Be sure to look for *Creating a Healthy Life, Seven Secrets of a Happy Life*, and a full-length Howard Murad autobiography to be published soon in eBook form.

ABOUT THE AUTHOR

A PRACTITIONER NOT just of medicine but of the philosophy of health, Howard Murad, M.D., focuses on overall well-being rather than spot treatment of individual conditions or diseases. The objective of his Inclusive Health approach is to help people live healthier, happier, and more successful lives by reawakening the vigor and creativity of their youth. Following his own advice, Dr. Murad is enjoying a second career as an artist. The spectacular paintings seen throughout this book are his own. Dr. Murad is the author of *The Water Secret* and *Creating a Healthy Life* as well as the *Health and Happiness* and *Surviving Cultural Stress* series.